# *The* Power *of*
# LEADERSHIP

*Devotionals of Wisdom
for Being an Effective Leader*

RACINE, WI

*The Power of Leadership*

ISBN: 979-8-88898-165-8 - *Paperback*
ISBN: 979-8-88898-166-5 - *Hardcover*
ISBN: 979-8-88898-167-2 - *Ebook*
Copyright © 2025 by John C. Maxwell & Honor Books, Racine, WI

Cover design by Faille Schmitz.

# INTRODUCTION

---

Powerful leaders are readers! Even those who don't read widely read wisely. They often clip articles and quotes to file for future use, which has been a practice of mine for more than thirty years.

Over the years, I have often been asked to share my quote collection. *The Power of Leadership* is my fulfillment of those requests for material on leadership. Long ago, learned that if you want to quote like a leader, you must note like a leader. In this book, you will find great material to help you build your leadership power. So be ready to take some notes and file some quotes!

JOHN C. MAXWELL

# THE DEFINITION

> *Leadership is influence.*
>
> ## JOHN C. MAXWELL

This is my favorite definition of leadership. It's a simple, straightforward, one-word description that places leadership within everyone's reach. All of us can exercise a certain degree of influence on someone, at some point, in some place.

Leadership isn't about titles, positions, or flowcharts. It's about one life influencing another.

*If the highest aim of a captain were to preserve his ship, he would keep it in port forever.*

### THOMAS AQUINAS

*Do not let kindness and truth leave you; bind them around your neck, write them on the tablet of your heart. So you will find favor and a good reputation in the sight of God and man.*

### PROVERBS 3:3-4 NASB

*It is better to lead from behind and to put others in front, especially when you celebrate victory when nice things occur. You take the front line when there is danger. Then people will appreciate your leadership.*

### NELSON MANDELA

## POWER UP

*What type of influence do you want to have as a leader?*

_____

_____

_____

_____

_____

# INTEGRITY OR BUST

---

> *Character is power.*
>
> **BOOKER T. WASHINGTON**

T he first lesson we must each learn is that broad leadership is built from deep character.

An infrastructure of great character is essential to support great conduct. The trust and involvement of our followers will be parallel to the level of our won character.

*I am not afraid of an army of lions led by a sheep;*
*I am afraid of an army of sheep led by a lion.*

## ALEXANDER THE GREAT

*. . . we also glory in our sufferings, because we know that*
*suffering produces perseverance; perseverance, character;*
*and character, hope.*

## ROMANS 5:3-4 NIV

*Goodness is about character—integrity, honesty, kindness,*
*generosity, moral courage, and the like. More than any-*
*thing else, it is about how we treat other people.*

## DENNIS PRAGER

## POWER UP

*What aspects of your character most fuel your leadership?*
*What areas could you grow in?*

# TRUE GREATNESS

---

> *Use power to help people. For we are given power not to advance our own purposes, nor to make a great show in the world, nor a name. There is but one just use of power, and it is to serve people.*
>
> ## GEORGE BUSH

George Bush was right. We abuse our power when we utilize it for self-gain. One of the buzzwords of the '90s was the word "empower." It simply means to give your power away. This is what people are longing for their leaders to do. This truth is echoed by Jesus in Matthew 20:26: *". . . whoever wishes to become great among you shall be your servant."*

*When your values are clear to you, making decisions be-comes easier.*

## ROY E. DISNEY

*. . . whoever wants to become great among you must be your servant . . .*

## MATTHEW 20:26 NIV

*The purpose of human life is to serve, and to show compassion and the will to help others.*

## ALBERT SCHWEITZER

## POWER UP

*What about servanthood makes it a desirable trait for a leader?*

_____

_____

_____

_____

_____

# THE THINKER AND THE DOER

---

*Failure can be divided into those who thought and never did and into those who did and never thought.*

REVEREND W. A. NANCE

Someone once told me that the world has two kinds of people: thinkers and doers. They then said, "the thinkers need to do more, and the doers need to think more." I have always tried to do both—reflect and act. When I have combined the two, I have greatly reduced the odds of failure.

*Leadership is solving problems. The day soldiers stop bringing you their problems is the day you have stopped leading them. They have either lost confidence that you can help or concluded you do not care. Either case is a failure of leadership.*

## COLIN POWELL

*. . . prove yourselves doers of the word, and not just hearers who deceive themselves.*

## JAMES 1:22 NASB

*The cautious seldom err.*

## CONFUCIUS

## POWER UP

*Which side do you tend to err on: the thinker or the doer?*

_____

_____

_____

_____

_____

# COACH AND COMRADE

> *Leaders must be close enough to relate to others,*
> *but far enough ahead to motivate them.*
>
> JOHN C. MAXWELL

I have always believed this principle. It beautifully combines the necessity of both relationship and vision. I must live with the people to understand them and earn their trust. However, I am only their "buddy" if that's all I do. To be a leader, I must live with God and move with Him beyond where the people are. If they are to follow me, I must be ahead of them.

*Go as far as you can see; when you get there, you'll be able to see farther.*

## J. P. MORGAN

*Brethren, be followers together of me, and mark them which walk so as ye have us for an ensample.*

## PHILIPPIANS 3:17

*Leadership is unlocking people's potential to become better.*

## BILL BRADLEY

## POWER UP

*How do you motivate others by example?*

_____

_____

_____

_____

_____

# MAKING THE DREAM WORK

---

> *Leadership is the capacity to translate vision into reality.*
>
> WARREN G. BENNIS

**M**ost of us learn the hard way that leadership is not merely having a vision. Anyone can dream. Effective leadership is knowing how to lay down the action steps for yourself and the organization so that the vision can be realized. This requires us to be practical and to understand the process along the way.

*The quality of a leader is reflected in the standards they set for themselves.*

## RAY KROC

*Where there is no vision, the people perish . . .*

## PROVERBS 29:18

*Without initiative, leaders are simply workers in leadership positions.*

## BO BENNETT

## POWER UP

*What are some steps you've taken to realize a dream? How would you advise another in their pursuit?*

# PEOPLE, NOT PAWNS

---

*You manage things; you lead people.*

**GRACE MURRAY HOPPER**
**ADMIRAL, US NAVY, RETIRED**

I must have articulated this principle a hundred times during my years as a pastor. People don't want to be managed, organized, stereotyped, tagged, or filed. That's what you do with things in an office. People are dynamic and must be led through love and relationship.

*Leadership is having a compelling vision, a comprehensive plan, relentless implementation, and talented people working together.*

## ALAN MULALLY

*Humble yourselves in the presence of the Lord, and He will exalt you.*

## JAMES 4:10 NASB

*No man will make a great leader who wants to do it all himself or get all the credit for doing it.*

## ANDREW CARNEGIE

## POWER UP

*How do you maintain a warmth of relationship with those under your leadership?*

_____

_____

_____

_____

_____

# BEING BIG ENOUGH

> *A man must be big enough to admit his mistakes,*
> *smart enough to profit from them,*
> *and strong enough to correct them.*

One of the least talked about prerequisites for leadership is a strong sense of personal security. Without it, I sabotage myself and my organization. With it, I can handle mistakes with perspective, and have the ability to admit them, profit from them and correct them.

*A good leader takes a little more than his share of the blame, a little less than his share of the credit.*

## ARNOLD H. GLASOW

*For the Lord takes delight in his people; he crowns the humble with victory.*

## PSALM 149:4 NIV

*The task of the leader is to get his people from where they are to where they have not been.*

## HENRY KISSINGER

## POWER UP

*What is a mistake that you're glad you made, in retrospect, due to the value of the lesson?*

# DON'T BE A PEOPLE-PLEASER

One of the weaknesses of many of today's leaders is our compulsion to take surveys. It happens in politics, and it happens in churches. A leader must go beyond being a people-pleaser to being a God-pleaser. If our need for the people's affirmation exceeds our need for God's affirmation, we're in trouble. Leadership sometimes means doing what's unpopular.

*If a window of opportunity appears,*
*don't pull down the shade.*

## TOM PETERS

*Am I now trying to win the approval of human beings, or*
*of God? Or am I trying to please people? If I were still*
*trying to please people, I would not be a servant of Christ.*

## GALATIANS 1:10 NIV

*Leadership is an opportunity to serve.*
*It is not a trumpet call to self-importance.*

## J. DONALD WALTERS

## POWER UP

*What idea have you held back on because it might be unpopular?*

# THE RECIPE FOR GREATNESS

> *You are the same today that you are going to be five years from now except for two things: the people with whom you associate and the books you read.*
>
> **CHARLES "TREMENDOUS" JONES**

I read this statement by Charlie Jones years ago, and I've become more convinced of its truth as time goes by. If we plan to become great, we must determine to expose ourselves to great books and great people. Their input will influence our growth more than anything else. Choose both wisely.

*Reading is to the mind what exercise is to the body.*

### JOSEPH ADDISON

*. . . so that I may come to you with joy, by God's will, and in your company be refreshed.*

### ROMANS 15:32 NIV

*Affirmation without discipline is the beginning of delusion.*

### JIM ROHN

## POWER UP

*What great people or great books have been milestones of growth in your life?*

_____

_____

_____

_____

_____

# THE CREAM ALWAYS RISES

*No matter what size the bottle, the cream always came to the top.*

**CHARLES WILSON
PRESIDENT, GE**

Pastoring in the Midwest, I quickly learned that people are somewhat like fresh milk from a cow. At first glance it all looks the same. But eventually the cream rises to the top. Similarly you'll find that given time, the "movers and shakers" naturally rise to the top. Simply watch and wait.

*Good leadership consists of showing average people how to do the work of superior people.*

## JOHN D. ROCKEFELLER

*For You bless the righteous person, Lord, You surround him with favor as with a shield.*

## PSALM 5:12 NASB

*Leadership consists of picking good men and helping them do their best.*

## CHESTER W. NIMITZ

# POWER UP

*What are some early indicators of a potential "mover or shaker"?*

# THE RISK OF SAFETY

---

*A ship in a harbor is safe, but that is not
what ships were built for.*

We've all seen this statement on a plaque or poster somewhere. What a great reminder it is that safety, security, and survival are not meaningful goals for our lives. If we're going to get anywhere, we're going to have to risk venturing into the unknown. Life is about adventure, not maintenance.

*Leadership is practiced not so much in words as in attitude and in actions.*

### HAROLD S. GENEEN

*Therefore, since we also have such a great cloud of witnesses surrounding us, let's rid ourselves of every obstacle and the sin which so easily entangles us, and let's run with endurance the race that is set before us . . .*

### HEBREWS 12:1 NASB

*Obstacles are things a person sees when he takes his eyes off his goal.*

### E. JOSEPH COSSMAN

## POWER UP

*What area of your life would most benefit from stepping out of your comfort zone?*

_____

_____

_____

_____

_____

# COMMUNICATE OR CRUMBLE

*You can have brilliant ideas, but if you can't get them across, your ideas won't get you anywhere.*

LEE IACOCCA

I discovered this truth as I observed my staff attempting to cast a vision to the people in their departments. Ideas alone can't harness a group of people. We can only move to accomplish a goal when the vision is cast clearly, creatively, and consistently.

*Where there is no vision, there is no hope.*

## GEORGE WASHINGTON CARVER

*Commit to the Lord whatever you do, and he will establish your plans.*

## PROVERBS 16:3 NIV

*Clarity affords focus.*

## THOMAS LEONARD

## POWER UP

*What are two essential elements of clear vision casting?*

_____

_____

_____

_____

_____

# IF THE SHOE FITS

> *Asking "Who ought to be the boss?" is like asking "Who ought to be the tenor in the quartet?" Obviously, the man who can sing tenor.*
>
> HENRY FORD

I love the simple, unpretentious logic, of Henry Ford. He cuts through the red tape of human politics, suggesting that leadership isn't a matter of tenure or title, but ability. The appropriate question is, "Who can get the job done?"

*Effective leadership is putting first things first. Effective management is discipline, carrying it out.*

### STEPHEN COVEY

*To one he gave five talents, to another, two, and to another, one, each according to his own ability; and he went on his journey.*

### MATTHEW 25:15 NASB

*Hold yourself responsible for a higher standard than anybody expects of you. Never excuse yourself.*

### HENRY WARD BEECHER

## POWER UP

*What natural talent has been most instrumental in your leadership?*

# ATTITUDE WITH ALTITUDE

> *Nothing great was ever achieved without enthusiasm.*
>
> RALPH WALDO EMERSON

I am an attitude nut. I just happen to believe that an enthusiastic attitude places a leader above his peers, opens his mind to creativity, and provides motivation to his people.

"Enthusiasm" is taken from two root words: "*en*" and "*theos*," meaning "God within." If we have God living on the inside of us, we ought to be enthusiastic!

*How we think shows through in how we act. Attitudes are mirrors of the mind. They reflect thinking.*

### DAVID JOSEPH SCHWARTZ

*And whatsoever ye do, do it heartily, as to the Lord, and not unto men . . .*

### COLOSSIANS 3:23

*Everyone who's ever taken a shower has an idea. It's the person who gets out of the shower, dries off and does something about it who makes a difference.*

### NOLAN BUSHNELL

## POWER UP

*How do you believe others would describe your attitude on any given day?*

_____

_____

_____

_____

_____

# DELEGATE WELL

---

I have always tried to lead my staff this way: I select and salary my team based upon ability and productivity. When I place a leader in a position that fits his or her abilities, it is apparent in the overall quality of their work. That done, I leave them to reach the goals we've set in whatever way they choose. I don't care so much how they get to the goal, as long as they reach it!

*What helps people, helps business.*

## LEO BURNETT

*Moses listened to his father-in-law and did everything he said. He chose capable men from all Israel and made them leaders of the people, officials over thousands, hundreds, fifties and tens.*

## EXODUS 18:24-25 NIV

*Honor bespeaks worth. Confidence begets trust. Service brings satisfaction. Cooperation proves the quality of leadership.*

## JAMES CASH PENNEY

## POWER UP

*How would you rate your ability to delegate?*

# LEADING BY EXAMPLE

---

*The single most important factor in determining the climate of an organization is the top executive.*

CHARLES GALLOWAY

E verything rises and falls on leadership. Once a leader has been directing an organization (or church) for two years or more, the personality, atmosphere, and problems of that organization are a result of his leadership. When you see him, you see the organization.

*Example is leadership.*

## ALBERT SCHWEITZER

*Be diligent to present yourself approved to God as a worker who does not need to be ashamed, accurately handling the word of truth.*

## 2 TIMOTHY 2:15 NASB

*Great companies in the way they work, start with great leaders.*

## STEVE BALLMER

## POWER UP

*What characteristics do you admire in other leaders and wish to emulate?*

# STAND IN THE GAP

---

> *You must live with people to know their problems, and live with God in order to solve them.*
>
> ## P. T. FORSYTH

This truism combines two very important ingredients for a leader. A leader is called to stand in the gap between the people and God. We must be close enough to the people to represent them (their needs and struggles) before God. At the same time, we must be close enough to God to represent Him (His answers and direction) before the people. This is the key balancing act before us.

*The real leader has no need to lead—he is content to point the way.*

## HENRY MILLER

*Commit thy way unto the Lord; trust also in him; and he shall bring it to pass.*

## PSALMS 37:5

*Strong convictions precede great actions.*

## JAMES FREEMAN CLARKE

## POWER UP

*What are conscious ways you represent God in your relationship with those you are leading?*

_____

_____

_____

_____

_____

# THE VALUE OF EXPERIENCE

*Reportedly, IBM's Tom Watson was asked if he was going to fire an employee who made a mistake that cost IBM $600,000. He said, "No, I just spent $600,000 training him. Why would I want somebody to hire his experience?"*

Tom Watson's response provides insight to leaders who are tempted to let a staff member go after a mistake or failure. If their mistake was not immoral or fundamentally undermining to the direction of the organization, we might do well to keep them. Why not view it as a learning experience, and consider it an investment in the future?

*Don't find fault, find a remedy.*

### HENRY FORD

*Brethren, if a man be overtaken in a fault, ye which are spiritual, restore such a one in the spirit of meekness . . .*

### GALATIANS 6:1

*Management is about arranging and telling. Leadership is about nurturing and enhancing.*

### TOM PETERS

## POWER UP

*How do you handle the mistakes of others?*

# LIVE AND LEARN

---

> *Failure is the opportunity to begin again,*
> *more intelligently.*
>
> HENRY FORD

Once again, Henry Ford's simplicity strikes me. Failure was never final to him, nor was it fatal. Like his contemporary, Thomas Edison, he expected failures on the way to success. It was all part of the learning process. He allowed failure to tutor him, then he continued on down the path that is much smarter and wiser.

*To succeed, one must be creative and persistent.*

### JOHN H. JOHNSON

*You need to persevere so that when you have done the will of God, you will receive what he has promised.*

### HEBREWS 10:36 NIV

*Think little goals and expect little achievements. Think big goals and win big success.*

### DAVID JOSEPH SCHWARTZ

## POWER UP

*How do you react to failure?*

# DON'T SETTLE FOR LESS

> *Show me a thoroughly satisfied man,*
> *and I will show you a failure.*
>
> THOMAS EDISON

I find it terribly difficult to understand a person who is so satisfied with their present accomplishments that they have no desire to risk attempting something new. There is nothing wrong with spiritual contentment with our possessions and resources, but each of us should carry to our grave a holy dissatisfaction with our achievements.

*If you have ideas, you have the main asset you need, and there isn't any limit to what you can do with your business and your life. Ideas are any man's greatest asset.*

## HARVEY S. FIRESTONE

*For God has not given us a spirit of timidity, but of power and love and discipline.*

## 2 TIMOTHY 1:7 NASB

*There are risks and costs to action. But they are far less than the long range risks of comfortable inaction.*

## JOHN F. KENNEDY

## POWER UP

*How do you shake yourself out of your own comfort zone?*

# EYE FOR POTENTIAL

> *I will have no man work for me who has not the capacity to become a partner.*
>
> J. C. PENNEY

I have heard many single women say they won't date a man who isn't a potential marriage partner. They don't want to waste their time with unproductive emotional entanglements. J. C. Penney looked at employees the same way. He looked for the raw ability in all of them—the capacity to rise in the organization. If necessary, it is wise to create a position for those kind of people when you find them!

*Making good decisions is a crucial skill at every level.*

## PETER DRUCKER

*Do not give dogs what is sacred; do not throw your pearls to pigs. If you do, they may trample them under their feet, and turn and tear you to pieces.*

## MATTHEW 7:6 NIV

*Get the best people and train them well.*

## SCOTT MCNEALY

## POWER UP

*How do you draw out the potential in others?*

# CHOOSE WISELY

---

*Here lies a man who knew how to enlist the service of better men than himself.*

**ANDREW CARNEGIE'S TOMBSTONE**

I am drawn to Carnegie's humility, as well as his talent. He didn't try to do it all or own it all. He once said, "I owe whatever success I have achieved, by the large, to my ability to surround myself with people who are smarter than I am."

He knew his own limitations, but that only spurred him on to find associates who didn't have the same ones.

*Be the chief but never the lord.*

## LAO TZU

*Two are better than one; because they have a good reward for their labour. For if they fall, the one will lift up his fellow: but woe to him that is alone when he falleth; for he hath not another to help him up.*

## ECCLESIASTES 4:9-10

*Our business in life is not to get ahead of others, but to get ahead of ourselves.*

## E. JOSEPH COSSMAN

## POWER UP

*How do you curate your inner circle?*

# MAKE YOUR OWN LICK

*Luck is the residue of design.*

**BRANCH RICKEY**

P eople talk a lot about good luck and bad luck. I believe, however, that Branch Rickey was right. Very few outcomes in this cause and effect world are due to chance. Someone has said, "Good luck is what happens when opportunity meets preparation."

*Give whatever you are doing and whoever you are with the gift of your attention.*

## JIM ROHN

*Be very careful, then, how you live—not as unwise but as wise, making the most of every opportunity, because the days are evil.*

## EPHESIANS 5:15-16 NIV

*The amount of good luck coming your way depends on your willingness to act.*

## BARBARA SHER

## POWER UP

*What preparations do you make for opportunities of "good luck"?*

# YOU HAVE TO START SOMEWHERE

> *All glory comes from daring to begin.*
>
> EUGENE F. WARE

To begin a task is usually the toughest step. Indeed, the journey of a thousand miles begins with a single step, but I've found that step keeps most people stationary. The gear of attempting something big immobilizes them. This is why beginning is half the battle, and why all glory comes from daring to begin.

*No matter how carefully you plan your goals they will never be more than pipe dreams unless you pursue them with gusto.*

## W. CLEMENT STONE

*Though thy beginning was small, yet thy latter end should greatly increase.*

## JOB 8:7

*If you care enough for a result, you will most certainly attain it.*

## WILLIAM JAMES

## POWER UP

*What first step have you been holding back on taking?*

_____

_____

_____

_____

_____

# WORTHY INVESTMENT

---

> *Don't spend a dollar's worth of time
> on a 10-cent decision.*

I try to invest the appropriate amount of time and mental energy into every decision I make. Visualize a scale: on one side is the weight of how much the decision will cost. On the other, how much it will benefit. Balance each decision's potential benefit with its actual cost.

*The sharp employ the sharp.*

## DOUGLAS WILLIAM JERROLD

*Suppose one of you wants to build a tower. Won't you first sit down and estimate the cost to see if you have enough money to complete it?*

## LUKE 14:28 NIV

*The function of leadership is to produce more leaders, not more followers.*

## RALPH NADER

## POWER UP

*Do you know when to call it quits on an investment?*

# KEEP IT COOL

---

> *Nothing gives one person so much advantage*
> *over another as to remain always cool*
> *and unruffled under all circumstances.*
>
> **THOMAS JEFFERSON**

Poise comes through maturity. When we get it, and can keep it under pressure, we will have a decided advantage over others. Panicking usually has a negative effect on a situation, but remaining calm and cool enables us to think and act more intelligently. Make it your ambition to never panic.

*Never be in a hurry; do everything quietly and in a calm spirit. Do not lose your inner peace for anything whatsoever, even if your whole world seems upset.*

## SAINT FRANCIS DE SALES

*Whoever is patient has great understanding, but one who is quick-tempered displays folly.*

## PROVERBS 14:29 NIV

*The supreme quality for leadership is unquestionably integrity. Without it, no real success is possible, no matter whether it is on a section gang, a football field, in an army, or in an office.*

## DWIGHT D. EISENHOWER

## POWER UP

*How do you keep your cool when pressure rises?*

# STUDENT OF LIFE

---

> *The moment you stop learning, you stop leading.*
>
> RICK WARREN

L eaders are learners. Once a person feels they have a firm grasp on all the answers, they have quit being teachable and will soon cease from leading. Their thoughts and methods will become dated, and eventually stale. Good leaders are hungry for learning, all the way to the grave.

*The very exercise of leadership fosters capacity for it.*

## CYRIL FALLS

*A wise person will hear and increase in learning, and a person of understanding will acquire wise counsel . . .*

## PROVERBS 1:5 NASB

*Leadership is not about a title or a designation. It's about impact, influence and inspiration. Impact involves getting results, influence is about spreading the passion you have for your work, and you have to inspire team-mates and customers.*

## ROBIN S. SHARMA

# POWER UP

*Do you have an appetite for learning?*
*How could you improve your diet?*

# ABOVE AND BEYOND

---

*A person who is successful has simply formed
the habit of doing things that unsuccessful people
will not do.*

---

Whatever business field you may have chosen, success will follow you if you will consistently do the things and provide the services that others refuse to do and fail to provide.

This makes for outstanding leadership and creates a demand for you and what you do.

*The key to successful leadership today is influence,
not authority.*

## KEN BLANCHARD

*Therefore humble yourselves under the mighty hand of God,
so that He may exalt you at the proper time . . .*

## 1 PETER 5:6 NASB

*Men make history and not the other way around. In periods where there is no leadership, society stands still. Progress occurs when courageous, skillful leaders seize the opportunity to change things for the better.*

## HARRY S. TRUMAN

# POWER UP

*What are some ways you push yourself to go above and beyond?*

# DO OR DIE

Our reputation is obviously constructed from our track record, not our intentions. As I travel, I meet pastors and businessmen from all over the country. Many of them know the right principles, talk the correct language, and lay the proper plans. Unfortunately, it takes more than that to build a dynamic church or a profitable business. Success is about what we've produced, not what we've planned.

*The test of leadership is not to put greatness into human-ity, but to elicit it, for the greatness is already there.*

## JAMES BUCHANAN

*A good name is rather to be chosen than great riches, and loving favour rather than silver and gold.*

## PROVERBS 22:1

*Action is the foundational key to all success.*

## PABLO PICASSO

## POWER UP

*What most often prevents you from pulling the trigger on a plan?*

_____

_____

_____

_____

_____

# TRAILBLAZING

---

> *If you want to succeed, you should strike out on new paths rather than travel the worn paths of accepted success.*
>
> JOHN D. ROCKEFELLER

I t's amazing to me that the level of Olympic competition at the turn of the twentieth century are now the levels at which junior high school students compete. Why is that? During the last one-hundred years, athletes have invariably discovered new ways to run faster, jump higher, and throw farther. Success, therefore, has meant not merely doing what previous champions have done but pioneering new methods.

*In order to carry a positive action we must develop here a positive vision.*

### DALAI LAMA

*Give careful thought to the paths for your feet and be steadfast in all your ways. Do not turn to the right or the left; keep your foot from evil.*

### PROVERBS 4:26-27 NIV

*Leadership is not a popularity contest; it's about leaving your ego at the door. The name of the game is to lead without a title.*

### ROBIN S. SHARMA

## POWER UP

*Is trailblazing an exciting or stressful prospect in your mind? What keeps you from branching off the beaten path?*

# RISE TO THE CHALLENGE

> *You cannot push anyone up the ladder unless he is willing to climb a little.*
>
> ANDREW CARNEGIE

No one can succeed for you. Success isn't a gift to be given away. Believe me, I have tried many times to "jump start" one of my staff, just to help them make it beyond where they might have gone alone. Some responded and rose to the challenge. Others, despite my optimism, were unable or unwilling to climb a step up the ladder.

*The growth and development of people is the highest calling of leadership.*

## HARVEY S. FIRESTONE

*The sluggard will not plow by reason of the cold; therefore shall he beg in harvest, and have nothing.*

## PROVERBS 20:4

*True leadership lies in guiding others to success. In ensuring that everyone is performing at their best, doing the work they are pledged to do and doing it well.*

## BILL OWENS

## POWER UP

*How do you try to "jumpstart" those you are leading?*

# BUILDING TOGETHER

---

*People support what they help create.*

I'm convinced that the surest way to establish a sense of ownership among your constituency is to involve them in the creative process all along the way. You might be able to reach a goal faster on your own, but when you get there you will be just that — on your own. Slow down, and take your people along.

*Leadership is a privilege to better the lives of others.
It is not an opportunity to satisfy personal greed.*

### MWAI KIBAKI

*But we ask you, brothers and sisters, to recognize those
who diligently labor among you . . . that you regard them
very highly in love because of their work. Live in peace
with one another.*

### 1 THESSALONIANS 5:12-13 NASB

*I've always maintained—a captain is only as good as his
team. It is not about my leadership, it is not about me.*

### GAUTAM GAMBHIR

## POWER UP

*How do you invite others to build with you?*

_____

_____

_____

_____

_____

# THE BEGINNING OF WISDOM

---

> *It's what you learn after you know it all that counts.*
>
> JOHN WOODEN

John Wooden has been there. Here's a coach who could have easily assumed he knew it all. It's at that point, however, that the greatest lessons and most profound discoveries are found. Someone once said: "We only learn what we already know." When we get beyond a superficial understanding of an idea or concept is when the truth really sinks in.

*At the heart of great leadership is a curious mind, heart, and spirit.*

## CHIP CONLEY

*Do not be wise in your own eyes;*
*fear the Lord and shun evil.*

## PROVERBS 3:7 NIV

*Humility is the solid foundation of all virtues.*

## CONFUCIUS

## POWER UP

*What are some subjects you could delve deeper into understanding as a leader?*

_____

_____

_____

_____

_____

# PRESSURE MAKES DIAMONDS

> *A good leader is a guy who can step on
> your toes without messing up your shine.*

I've seen some of the best pastors and business executives in the country at work. They all seem to have the keen ability to speak the truth, to lay out the imperatives, and to communicate the marching orders to their people. At the same time, they do so with such warmth and understanding, with such humor and sensitivity that no one feels pushed. They actually like the experience and feel they are better for it.

*Leadership should be born out of the understanding of the
needs of those who would be affected by it.*

## MARIAN ANDERSON

*A soft answer turneth away wrath:
but grievous words stir up anger.*

## PROVERBS 15:1

*Constant, gentle pressure is my preferred technique
for leadership, guidance, and coaching.*

## DANNY MEYER

## POWER UP

*How do you maintain a healthy level of pressure?*

_____

_____

_____

_____

_____

# DOING VS BEING

> *We are what we repeatedly do; excellence then is not an act, but a habit.*
>
> ARISTOTLE

Success is not an event. It is an ongoing process we engage in, time and time again. Aristotle says it in a profound way. Anyone can succeed once or twice. And, anyone can fail or lose a battle or two along the way. What we must focus on is the habit of excellence; practicing success, repeatedly, day after day.

*Character matters; leadership descends from character.*

## RUSH LIMBAUGH

*If the axe is dull and he does not sharpen its edge, then he must exert more strength. Wisdom has the advantage of bringing success.*

## ECCLESIASTES 10:10 NASB

*Practice self-awareness, self-evaluation, and self-improvement. If we are aware that our manners—language, behavior, and actions—are measured against our values and principles, we are able to more easily embody the philosophy, leadership is a matter of how to be, not how to do.*

## FRANCES HESSELBEIN

## POWER UP

*What would you define as a habit of excellence?*

# EAGLE EYE

You've probably noticed this too. Unlike most birds, eagles don't fly in flocks. They don't simply fit in. They don't conform to the activities of their own kind. You cannot find them in huge clusters. They are flying along, ahead of and higher than the other birds. Leaders are like eagles.

*One thing that somebody told me is that leadership is a lonely role—some people can do it, and some people can't.*

## KYRIE IRVING

*"Enter through the narrow gate. For wide is the gate and broad is the road that leads to destruction, and many enter through it. But small is the gate and narrow the road that leads to life, and only a few find it."*

## MATTHEW 7:13-14 NIV

*We live in a society obsessed with public opinion. But leadership has never been about popularity.*

## MARCO RUBIO

## POWER UP

*Do you ever find yourself lonely in your role of leadership? How do you combat this feeling?*

# TAKE ACTION

---

*A man who has to be convinced to act before he acts is not a man of action.*

GEORGES CLEMENCEAU

I can easily lose patience with people whom I continually have to persuade before they will make a move. People of action don't need a pep talk every time their organization needs to take a risk. I'm not suggesting we don't plan, but men of action often embrace the method that Tom Peters made popular: "Ready. Fire. Aim."

*Making good decisions is a crucial skill at every level.*

## PETER DRUCKER

*Say to the righteous that it will go well for them,
for they will eat the fruit of their actions.*

## ISAIAH 3:10 NASB

*Inaction breeds doubt and fear. Action breeds confidence
and courage. If you want to conquer fear, do not sit home
and think about it. Go out and get busy.*

## DALE CARNEGIE

## POWER UP

*How do you encourage others into action?*

_____

_____

_____

_____

_____

# EXPECTATION FOR EXCELLENCE

> *Be a yardstick of quality. Some people aren't used to an environment where excellence is expected.*
>
> STEVE JOBS

Steve Jobs, the founder of Apple, understood as well as anyone what it takes to build excellence into people. He knew that most people don't pursue excellence naturally. Pioneering a new corporation, he recognized that he had the opportunity to set a standard from the very beginning. Ultimately, he understood that this could only take place if he became the example of the quality he desired. He had to be the yardstick for excellence.

*Perfection is not attainable, but if we chase perfection we can catch excellence.*

## VINCE LOMBARDI

*All hard work brings a profit,
but mere talk leads only to poverty.*

## PROVERBS 14:23 NIV

*A good objective of leadership is to help those who are doing poorly to do well and to help those who are doing well to do even better.*

## JIM ROHN

## POWER UP

*What is the standard have you set for quality
for those under your leadership?*

_____

_____

_____

_____

_____

# LONELINESS IN LEADERSHIP

This little word picture is pregnant with meaning. If a man wants to lead the orchestra, he must first make a solitary decision. He cannot drift along with the crowd, nor can he pay attention to the crowd's response to his leading. He must remain focused, and be willing to stand alone. He must give himself to the few who are cooperating with him, not the masses who are looking on. Finally, even if he yearns for the crowd's applause, that cannot be his goal. His goal must be to lead his orchestra with excellence. The applause is a by-product.

*The biggest part of leadership is that you lead by example with your performance first and foremost.*

## JUDE BELLINGHAM

*Truly my soul waiteth upon God: from him cometh my salvation. He only is my rock and my salvation; he is my defence; I shall not be greatly moved.*

## PSALM 62:1-2

*Be able to be alone. Lose not the advantage of solitude, and the society of thyself.*

## THOMAS BROWNE

## POWER UP

*What effect does solitude have on you?*

_____

_____

_____

_____

_____

# NOTHING NEW
# UNDER THE SUN

*Congealed thinking is the forerunner of failure . . .
make sure you are always receptive to new ideas.*

**GEORGE CRANE**

I don't have to remind you that we live in a world of fast-paced change. We laugh at the fact that the U.S. Patent Office nearly closed down toward the end of the 19th century, because many felt that nothing new could be invented. Those who lead the pack today are those who are not only open to change, but to the new paradigms—whole new ways of looking at established facts. It was the Swiss who invented the digital wristwatch, but because their own watchmakers weren't open to a new idea—the Japanese have capitalized on it ever since.

*Positive leadership—conveying the idea that there is always a way forward—is so important, because that is what you are here for—to figure out how to move the organization forward.*

## ALAN MULALLY

*And we desire that each one of you demonstrate the same diligence . . . so that you will not be sluggish, but imitators of those who through faith and endurance inherit the promises.*

## HEBREWS 6:11-12 NASB

*For good ideas and true innovation, you need human inter-action, conflict, argument, debate.*

## MARGARET HEFFERNAN

## POWER UP

*What exercises or habits do you have in place to keep an open mind?*

# RIDING WITH NO TRAINING WHEELS

*It's okay to lend a helping hand—the challenge is getting people to let go of it.*

When something is freely offered for long enough, it is human nature to become dependent upon it. This is the reason behind the cry for welfare reform in our country. People get comfortable with the helping hand, and soon believe they can't live without it. Good leadership empowers people by providing the resources they need to get started, but the goal is to teach them how to be resourceful themselves.

*If you find a path with no obstacles,*
*it probably doesn't lead anywhere.*

## FRANK A. CLARK

*Therefore let us move beyond the elementary teachings*
*about Christ and be taken forward to maturity . . .*

## HEBREWS 6:1 NIV

*There is only one corner of the universe you can be certain*
*of improving, and that's your own self.*

## ALDOUS HUXLEY

## POWER UP

*What are some ways you regularly challenge yourself?*

# WALK THE WALK

---

*Being in power is like being a lady. If you have to tell people you are, you aren't.*

## MARGARET THATCHER

I love this quote from Margaret Thatcher of England. Any time our leadership is not obvious enough to those around us that it requires an explanation, we're in danger of losing it. If you must continually remind people that you are in control—someone else is likely assuming that role. Leadership should appear natural and be evident to all.

*A leader is one who, out of madness or goodness, volunteers to take upon himself the woe of the people. There are few men so foolish, hence the erratic quality of leadership in the world.*

### JOHN UPDIKE

*For the kingdom of God is not a matter of talk but of power.*

### 1 CORINTHIANS 4:20 NIV

*You learn far more from negative leadership than from positive leadership. Because you learn how not to do it. And, therefore, you learn how to do it.*

### NORMAN SCHWARZKOPF

## POWER UP

*Name some immediate tells of a leader.*

# AIM SMALL, MISS SMALL

> *I recommend you to take care of the minutes,*
> *for the hours will take care of themselves.*
>
> **LORD CHESTERFIELD**

Sometimes we miss the forest for the trees, and other times we miss the trees for the forest. When we only see the "big picture" and fail to see to it that the "minutes" are dealt with appropriately, we may miss accomplishing our big-picture goals. If we take care of the little things, we can build on that foundation, and eventually the hours will fall into place.

*Sometimes leadership is planting trees under whose shade you'll never sit. It may not happen fully till after I'm gone. But I know that the steps we're taking are the right steps.*

### JENNIFER GRANHOLM

*Take therefore no thought for the morrow: for the morrow shall take thought for the things of itself. Sufficient unto the day is the evil thereof.*

### MATTHEW 6:34

*Success is the sum of small efforts—repeated day in and day out.*

### ROBERT COLLIER

## POWER UP

*What are some areas you could focus your vision?*

# TRUE LEADERSHIP

---

> *An important question for leaders:*
> *"Am I building people, or building my dream*
> *and using people to do it?"*
>
> JOHN C. MAXWELL

Jack Hayford taught me something years ago. He said, "Our goal isn't to build a big church—but, to build big people." If we invest in people and develop them into mission-driven disciples, we will see our dream for the church accomplished. People quickly ascertain whether we are building them or using them.

*True urgent leadership doesn't drain people. It does the opposite. It energizes them. It makes them feel excited.*

## JOHN P. KOTTER

*. . . you also, like living stones, are being built into a spiritual house to be a holy priesthood, offering spiritual sacrifices acceptable to God through Jesus Christ.*

## 1 PETER 2:5 NIV

*The most important ingredient for the success of any company is the quality of its people, starting with its leadership team.*

## VIVEK RAMASWAMY

## POWER UP

*What efforts do you make to develop those you're working alongside?*

# HOLDING OUT FOR GOD'S BEST

---

*Learn to say no to the good so you can say yes to the best.*

JOHN C. MAXWELL

---

This is the battleground where I fight most often. I can easily distinguish between good and bad. Yet with my disposition, which wants to do everything, accomplish everything, and say yes to everything, I need accountability to choose between good and best. I have a "hatchet committee" that helps me say no to the good things along the way.

*The oldest, shortest words—'yes' and 'no'—are those which require the most thought.*

## PYTHAGORAS

*"But I say to you, take no oath at all, neither by heaven, for it is the throne of God, nor by the earth, for it is the footstool of His feet . . . But make sure your statement is, 'Yes, yes' or 'No, no'; anything beyond these is of evil origin."*

## MATTHEW 5:34-35, 37 NASB

*Leadership demands that we make tough choices.*

## ALAN AUTRY

## POWER UP

*Reflect on a time your patience for the best outcome paid off.*

_____

_____

_____

_____

_____

# WINNING HEARTS

---

> *Outstanding leaders appeal to the hearts of their followers, not their minds.*

I f you reflect on the most well-remembered political leaders in American history, you'll find men who were able to grip the hearts of the people: Lincoln, Roosevelt, Kennedy, Reagan. It's not about partisanship. It's about the ability to cast a vision, to empathize, to spark hope, to speak to the heart. It's not that these leaders didn't use logic; they just traveled beyond logic, to win the hearts of their audience.

*Lincoln's leadership is based on a number of precepts,*
*but my favorite one is that he acted in the name,*
*and for the good, of the people.*

## STEVEN SPIELBERG

*. . . they withdrew by themselves to a town called Beth-*
*saida, but the crowds learned about it and followed him.*
*He welcomed them and spoke to them about the kingdom*
*of God, and healed those who needed healing.*

## LUKE 9:10-11 NIV

*Leadership has a harder job to do than just choose sides.*
*It must bring sides together.*

## JESSE JACKSON

## POWER UP

*What characteristic of a leader wins hearts?*

# NO MAN IS AN ISLAND

*No man will make a great leader who wants to do it all himself, or to get all the credit for doing it.*

ANDREW CARNEGIE

L eadership, by definition, cannot be a one man show. If I don't possess the humility and desire to enable me to praise others and give them credit for their success, I'll be severely handicapped in my leadership. If my ego is so big that I insist on the applause, attention, and affirmation, potential partners will leave me alone; and I will end up with only what one person can accomplish.

*Unity is strength . . . when there is teamwork
and collaboration, wonderful things can be achieved.*

## MATTIE STEPANEK

*Do nothing out of selfish ambition or vain conceit.
Rather, in humility value others above yourselves . . .*

## PHILIPPIANS 2:3 NIV

*Great things in business are never done by one person.
They're done by a team of people.*

## STEVE JOBS

## POWER UP

*How do you ensure those under your leadership
receive recognition for their successes?*

# POWER TO THE PEOPLE

---

*Leadership is not wielding authority—*
*it's empowering people.*

**BECKY BRODIN**

---

Too many leaders make the mistake of thinking when they reach the top, it means they can use their position and power to force certain behaviors from their subordinates. We've all made the statement, "If I were in charge—things would be different . . ." However, leadership is not about a power trip, but about giving power to the people under you. It's about giving them the tools they need to do the job.

*If you don't understand that you work for your mislabeled 'subordinates', then you know nothing of leadership. You know only tyranny.*

## DEE HOCK

*Jesus called them together and said, "You know that the rulers of the Gentiles lord it over them, and their high officials exercise authority over them. Not so with you. Instead, whoever wants to become great among you must be your servant . . ."*

## MATTHEW 20:25-26 NIV

*Because power corrupts, society's demands for moral authority and character increase as the importance of the position increases.*

## JOHN ADAMS

## POWER UP

*Reflect on times you have felt empowered by another. How can you pass this encouragement along?*

# THE FOUNDATION OF CHARACTER

> *Every great institution is the lengthened shadow of a single man. His character determines the character of his organization.*
>
> RALPH WALDO EMERSON

Every organization reflects its leader. There would be no compassionate organization called The Salvation Army if not for William Booth. There would have been no Methodist Awakening if not for John Wesley. The modern missionary movement would not exist without William Carey. God doesn't look for masses, or even for committees, when He wants to do something—He looks for a leader.

*Leadership is an act of submission to God. To be a leader means listening to all kinds of people and situations. Out of that listening, we are hoping to discern the mind of God as best we can. This is the price of leadership—it's an act of sacrifice.*

## RICHARD FOSTER

*. . . we glory in tribulations also: knowing that tribulation worketh patience; and patience, experience; and experience, hope.*

## ROMANS 5:3-4

*Leadership is about making the right decision and the best decision before, sometimes, it becomes entirely popular.*

## MARTIN O'MALLEY

## POWER UP

*What building blocks of character do you base your life and leadership on?*

_____

_____

_____

_____

_____

# VISUAL LEADING

---

> *The most effective leadership is by example,*
> *not edict.*

N early 90% of how people learn is visual. It's what they see. Another 9% of our learning is verbal, or what we hear. About 1% is through our other senses. This alone explains why effective leadership is more caught than taught. People need to see a sermon, more than hear it, to really embrace it. A leader's credibility and his right to be followed are based on his life, as much as his lip.

*I think the greater responsibility, in terms of morality,
is where leadership begins.*

## NORMAN LEAR

*If one of you says to them, "Go in peace; keep warm and
well fed," but does nothing about their physical needs,
what good is it? In the same way, faith by itself, if it is not
accompanied by action, is dead.*

## JAMES 2:16-17 NIV

*A good example is far better than a good precept.*

## DWIGHT L. MOODY

## POWER UP

*What are some ways you intentionally model a good example?*

# WHO'S IN CHARGE HERE?

---

> *Whistler's Law: you never know who's right,*
> *but you always know who's in charge.*

I 've chuckled at the truth of this "law" more than once. There are indeed times when it's difficult to determine who is right. In fact, it may be an issue of subjective opinion in some cases. However, determining who's in charge is not nearly as difficult; just watch the people. When a tough decision needs to be made, who do they look to? Who do they trust? That's the person in charge.

*A leader is one who knows the way, goes the way,
and shows the way.*

## JOHN C. MAXWELL

*The wise prevail through great power, and those who
have knowledge muster their strength.*

## PROVERBS 24:5 NIV

*Leadership is hard to define and good leadership even
harder. But if you can get people to follow you to the ends
of the earth, you are a great leader.*

## INDRA NOOYI

## POWER UP

*What do people look to you for?*

# SIGHT WITHOUT VISION

*The most pathetic person in the world is someone who has sight but has no vision.*

HELEN KELLER

his is my favorite statement made by Helen Keller, a woman who was blind and deaf all of her life. She said this in response to the question: "What could be worse than being born without any sight?" Vision is non-negotiable for anyone who wants to succeed. It is the blueprint on the inside of a leader, before he ever sees the plan on the outside.

*I don't go by the rule book . . . I lead from the heart, not the head.*

## PRINCESS DIANA

*. . . having the understanding darkened, being alienated from the life of God through the ignorance that is in them, because of the blindness of their heart: who being past feeling have given themselves over unto lasciviousness, to work all uncleanness with greediness.*

## EPHESIANS 4:18-19

*I think that the greatest gift God ever gave man is not the gift of sight but the gift of vision. Sight is a function of the eyes, but vision is a function of the heart.*

## MYLES MUNROE

## POWER UP

*How do you maintain consistent focus on your pursuits?*

# LIVING WITH PURPOSE

---

> *If a man knows not what harbor he seeks,*
> *any wind is the right wind.*
>
> SENECA

This quote from Seneca is indicative of how so many people live their life. Not knowing what long-term direction they are headed for, they bounce around like a ball in a pinball machine. They live reactive lives based on what happens to them rather than proactive lives based on what values are in them. They live their life "by accident" rather than "on purpose."

*Efforts and courage are not enough without purpose
and direction.*

## JOHN F. KENNEDY

*The one who plants and the one who waters have one pur-
pose, and they will each be rewarded according to their
own labor.*

## 1 CORINTHIANS 3:8 NIV

*Our intention creates our reality.*

## WAYNE DYER

## POWER UP

*How do you stay proactive in living purposefully?*

# LEGACY

I n a word, the goal of a leader is to leave a "legacy." He wants to leave behind something permanent after he dies. He wants to have improved the lives of people in some corner of the world, or better yet, see them engaged in a cause that counts. This doesn't necessarily mean fame or wealth. It simply means people who continue in a mission because he has developed them.

*You don't lead by hitting people over the head—that's assault, not leadership.*

## DWIGHT D. EISENHOWER

*A good person leaves an inheritance to his grandchildren, And the wealth of a sinner is stored up for the righteous.*

## PROVERBS 13:22 NASB

*Legacy is not what I did for myself. It's what I'm doing for the next generation.*

## VITOR BELFORT

## POWER UP

*What legacy do you want to leave behind?*

_____

_____

_____

_____

_____

# THE HIGHEST HONOR

---

> *The highest compliment leaders can receive is the one that is given by the people who work for them.*

To me, success is being respected by those who are closest to me. I want to display integrity to those who see all my warts and wrinkles. I want to have the admiration of my family and my colleagues, the people who see me day in and day out. It's easy to be honored and esteemed by those who are far away and seldom seen. I want to be a hero at home.

*Knowledge will give you power, but character respect.*

## BRUCE LEE

*Be sure you know the condition of your flocks, give careful attention to your herds; for riches do not endure forever, and a crown is not secure for all generations.*

## PROVERBS 27:23-24 NIV

*Goodness is about character—integrity, honesty, kindness, generosity, moral courage, and the like. More than anything else, it is about how we treat other people.*

## DENNIS PRAGER

## POWER UP

*Reflect on a time someone under your leadership honored you in a meaningful way.*

# PRUNING MEANS GROWTH

> *It isn't the people you fire who make our life miserable, it's the people you don't.*
>
> **HARVEY MACKAY**

Throughout my ministry, I've been fascinated by the words Jesus spoke in John 15. Specifically, where He talks about pruning the vine so that the branches could continue to grow. I've met scores of pastors and leaders who are afraid to "prune" when it comes to their staff. They think it would not appear very "Christian." Quite the contrary. the concept is not only biblical, but if we don't practice it in our organizations, someday it may come back to haunt us.

*The culture of a workplace—an organization's values, norms and practices—has a huge impact on our happiness and success.*

## ADAM GRANT

*The wise woman builds her house, but with her own hands the foolish one tears hers down.*

## PROVERBS 14:1 NIV

*Give a lot, expect a lot, and if you don't get it, prune.*

## TOM PETERS

## POWER UP

*What part has pruning played in your personal growth?*

# LITERATE LEADERSHIP

> *Today a reader—tomorrow a leader.*
>
> MARGARET FULLER

One of the principles I've always tried to practice is to be well-read. I believe every meeting I enter without the preparation of good information is one where I can't easily assume my leadership role. Knowledge is power. As the leader, I must know more about the options in front of us, than my boards and committees. Reading helps my leading.

*To know that we know what we know, and to know that
we do not know what we do not know, that is true
knowledge.*

## NICOLAUS COPERNICUS

*The mind of the discerning acquires knowledge,
and the ear of the wise seeks knowledge.*

## PROVERBS 18:15 NASB

*The whole world opened to me when I learned to read.*

## MARY MCLEOD BETHUNE

## POWER UP

*What book has most influenced you as a leader?*

# LOUD AND CLEAR

---

> *The essence of leadership is a vision you articulate*
> *clearly and forcefully on every occasion.*
> *You can't blow an uncertain trumpet.*
>
> THEODORE HESBURGH

I 'll never forget hearing the "vision" of the Pepsi company a number of years ago: "The taste of Pepsi-Cola on the lips of everyone in the world." What a huge, overwhelming vision — yet how precise, measurable, and pointed it was. Everyone in the company knew it, and was harnessed to achieve it. Our vision must be heard until our people can embrace it.

*Give to us clear vision that we may know where to stand and what to stand for—because unless we stand for something, we shall fall for anything.*

**PETER MARSHALL**

*The Lord said, "I will certainly set you free for purposes of good . . ."*

**JEREMIAH 15:11 NASB**

*Good business leaders create a vision, articulate the vision, passionately own the vision, and relentlessly drive it to completion.*

**JACK WELCH**

## POWER UP

*What aspect of your personal vision could use a bump in volume?*

_____

_____

_____

_____

_____

# COMMITMENT TO LEADERSHIP

> *Leadership development is a lifetime journey—
> not a brief trip.*
>
> JOHN C. MAXWELL

I believe this now more than ever. About fifteen years ago, I thought I had a handle on leadership. No doubt, I did understand some significant leadership principles. But the more I grow, the more I recognize that my own leadership development will take a lifetime. It's not something we can pick up from a weekend conference. We must commit our lives to it.

*Strength and growth come only through continuous effort and struggle.*

## NAPOLEON HILL

*Commit thy way unto the Lord; trust also in him; and he shall bring it to pass.*

## PSALM 37:5

*The will to win, the desire to succeed, the urge to reach your full potential . . . these are the keys that will unlock the door to personal excellence.*

## CONFUCIUS

## POWER UP

*Have you had any instances where you questioned your commitment to leadership? How did you get through?*

# FOLLOW THE LEADER

*The test of leadership: turn around
and see if anyone is following you.*

This is the acid test of leadership. If you
want to evaluate your own leadership,
look at the people following you. Is anyone following? What kind of people do you attract?
Does your vision compel people to follow? Are they
committed to the vision? This is a simple series of
questions every leader should ask himself.

*Authenticity is the alignment of head, mouth, heart, and feet—thinking, saying, feeling, and doing the same thing—consistently. This builds trust, and followers love leaders they can trust.*

## LANCE SECRETAN

*Lead me in Your truth and teach me, for You are the God of my salvation; for You I wait all the day.*

## PSALM 25:5 NASB

*When you believe in your dream and your vision, then it begins to attract its own resources. No one was born to be a failure.*

## MYLES MUNROE

## POWER UP

*Why do people follow you? What type of people follow you?*

# YOU GET WHAT YOU PAY FOR

*If you pay peanuts, expect to get monkeys.*

I believe in having a staff that is "lean and mean" rather than "fat and sassy." As my last church grew, we were able to do so without adding any new staff over a long period of time. The reason? I paid my pastoral staff well, and I got the best. Because I paid them well, I was able to maintain a strong core, and as we grew they assumed multiple responsibilities. And they didn't have to work for peanuts.

*Employees who believe that management is concerned about them as a whole person—not just an employee— are more productive, more satisfied, more fulfilled.*

## ANNE M. MULCAHY

*A generous person will be prosperous, and one who gives others plenty of water will himself be given plenty.*

## PROVERBS 11:25 NASB

*Employers who recognize the importance of investing in their workforce have a more productive workforce, a more efficient workforce, a more loyal workforce, less turnover, and, in the private sector, more profitable.*

## VALERIE JARRETT

## POWER UP

*How do you ensure the people you lead feel valued?*

# THE POWER OF GOOD FAITH

*It is wonderful when the people believe in their leader:
but it is more wonderful when the leader believes in
the people!*

I t is difficult to say which must come first:
the leader believing in his people or vice
versa. However, I do know this: if a leader
begins to believe in his people, it is only a matter
of time before both occur. The fundamental step a
leader must take is to believe in his people and
communicate it to them. Don't ever settle for merely
impressing them.

*The true test of a leader is whether his followers will adhere to his cause from their own volition, enduring the most arduous hardships without being forced to do so, and remaining steadfast in the moments of greatest peril.*

### XENOPHON

*Let not your heart be troubled: ye believe in God, believe also in me.*

### JOHN 14:1

*Trust is to human relationships what faith is to gospel living. It is the beginning place, the foundation upon which more can be built. Where trust is, love can flourish.*

### BARBARA SMITH

## POWER UP

*How do you foster belief and trust in those you are leading?*

# THE STUFF OF GREATNESS

*If a leader demonstrates competency, genuine concern for others, and admirable character, people will follow.*

T. RICHARD CHASE

T. Richard Chase distills the basic components that followers look for in a leader. Are they competent? Do they really care for people? Do they possess strong character? Everything else is icing on the cake. Followers can endure a wide spectrum of differences in their leaders, but these three elements are non-negotiable.

*Be more concerned with your character than your reputation, because your character is what you really are, while your reputation is merely what others think you are.*

### JOHN WOODEN

*. . . we also celebrate in our tribulations, knowing that tribulation brings about perseverance; and perseverance, proven character; and proven character, hope; and hope does not disappoint . . .*

### ROMANS 5:3-5 NASB

*The foundation stones for a balanced success are honesty, character, integrity, faith, love and loyalty.*

### ZIG ZIGLAR

## POWER UP

*What makes a great leader?*

# OPPORTUNITY CALLS

---

*There is no security on this earth—only opportunity.*

DOUGLAS MACARTHUR

I think I first heard this statement as a quote from a general in Word War II. This world we live in does not offer any lasting security. It can't. What it does offer is trials, challenges, and a whole lot of opportunity. Our security can only be found in our obedience to God's call on our lives.

*Cowardice asks the question, is it safe? Expediency asks the question, is it politic? Vanity asks the question, is it popular? But conscience asks the question, is it right? And there comes a time when one must take a position that is neither safe, nor politic, nor popular, but one must take it because it is right.*

### MARTIN LUTHER KING, JR.

*On the day of prosperity be happy, but on the day of adversity consider: God has made the one as well as the other . . .*

### ECCLESIASTES 7:14 NASB

*A ship in port is safe, but that's not what ships are built for.*

### GRACE HOPPER

## POWER UP

*How do you maintain stability in an insecure world?*

# DELEGATE OR DECAY

Sometimes when we experience growth in our organization, we forget that our role as a leader must evolve too. The larger our organization grows, the less we can do by ourselves. We must commit ourselves to the task of oversight, or we will be overworked. While we must always model work, our chief task is empowering others to work.

*Life is a moving, breathing thing. We have to be willing to constantly evolve. Perfection is constant transformation.*

## NIA PEEPLES

*But grow in grace, and in the knowledge of our Lord and Saviour Jesus Christ. To him be glory both now and for ever. Amen.*

## 2 PETER 3:18

*As long as we are persistence in our pursuit of our deepest destiny, we will continue to grow. We cannot choose the day or time when we will fully bloom. It happens in its own time.*

## DENIS WAITLEY

## POWER UP

*Do you often find yourself stretched too thin? What changes can you make to ensure you have time to rest and recharge?*

# DREAM MADE REALITY

One of my favorite stories of possessing vision is about Walt Disney. Because Walt had passed away before the Grand Opening of Walt Disney World, Mrs. Disney was asked to appear on the stage at the opening ceremony. When she was introduced to come to the podium and greet the crowd, the master of ceremonies said to her, "Mrs. Disney—I just wish Walt could have seen this!"

Mrs. Disney simply responded, "He did!"

*Keep your dreams alive. Understand to achieve anything requires faith and belief in yourself, vision, hard work, determination, and dedication. Remember all things are possible for those who believe.*

## GAIL DEVERS

*Delight thyself also in the Lord: and he shall give thee the desires of thine heart.*

## PSALM 37:4

*The bravest are surely those who have the clearest vision of what is before them, glory and danger alike, and yet notwithstanding, go out to meet it.*

## THUCYDIDES

## POWER UP

*What's something you've "seen" that has yet to come to fruition?*

# FIRST THINGS FIRST

---

*Pay now, play later; play now, pay later.*

JOHN C. MAXWELL

I learned this simple truth from my dad. It's helped me to discard the notion of immediate gratification hundreds of times over the years. If I choose to pay the price for my dreams now, I'll enjoy the rewards of those dreams later. However, if I choose to play now, I may not have the opportunity for reward later. I'll be too busy paying the price.

*It was character that got us out of bed, commitment that moved us into action, and discipline that enabled us to follow through.*

## ZIG ZIGLAR

*We do not want you to become lazy, but to imitate those who through faith and patience inherit what has been promised.*

## HEBREWS 6:12 NIV

*The discipline of desire is the background of character.*

## JOHN LOCKE

## POWER UP

*Reflect on a time you put off immediate gratification for the bigger picture.*

# PLAN TO WIN

---

> *Failure to prepare is preparing to fail.*
>
> MIKE MURDOCK

Oh, I have found this to be true! I want to be prepared for every event I face. That's why I read. That's why I listen to audio media. It's why I study. It's why I dialogue with staff. I want to reduce the "surprise factor" as much as possible—life itself presents enough surprises, even for the thoroughly prepared. When I fail to prepare in one area, I set myself up for potential failure in other areas as well.

*Our goals can only be reached through a vehicle of a plan, in which we must fervently believe, and upon which we must vigorously act. There is no other route to success.*

## PABLO PICASSO

*The plans of the diligent lead to profit as surely as haste leads to poverty.*

## PROVERBS 21:5

*Leadership comes in small acts as well as bold strokes.*

## CARLY FIORINA

## POWER UP

*How do you prepare to win?*

_____

_____

_____

_____

_____

# REASONABLE CONFIDENCE

---

*A great man is always willing to be little.*

RALPH WALDO EMERSON

---

Great people have little use for fame or notoriety; they are consumed with productivity, not image. They do not feel the need to project their self-worth to anyone. They are content when the moment calls for them to be little, ordinary, or common—as long as the goal is achieved.

*Believe in yourself! Have faith in your abilities! Without a humble but reasonable confidence in your own powers you cannot be successful or happy.*

## NORMAN VINCENT PEALE

*". . . the Son of Man did not come to be served, but to serve, and to give his life as a ransom for many."*

## MATTHEW 20:28 NIV

*Do you wish to rise? Begin by descending. You plan a tower that will pierce the clouds? Lay first the foundation of humility.*

## SAINT AUGUSTINE

## POWER UP

*How do you keep your ego in check?*

# KNOWLEDGE IS POWER

> *As a rule . . . he (or she) who has the most information will have the greatest success in life.*
>
> **DISRAELI**

We've all heard it before: *knowledge is power.* Because there is doubtless truth to this axiom, I consume as much information as I possibly can in a variety of subjects relevant to me and my work. I have noticed that success follows the person who brings something to the table when the meeting begins; they are well-read and well-prepared. They never come across as ignorant in any subject.

*To acquire knowledge, one must study;*
*but to acquire wisdom, one must observe.*

## MARILYN VOS SAVANT

*The fear of the Lord is the beginning of knowledge;*
*fools despise wisdom and instruction.*

## PROVERBS 1:7 NASB

*Knowledge is power. Information is liberating. Education*
*is the premise of progress, in every society, in every family.*

## KOFI ANNAN

## POWER UP

*How do you outwork this statement in your life?*

_____

_____

_____

_____

_____

# GROW WITH THE FLOW

---

*Have confidence that if you have done a little thing well, you can do a bigger thing well too.*

### STOREY

L ife is full of graduations. In each stage of our journey, God has planned junctions where we will either pass or fail the quiz life has presented. Not only does God promise greater opportunities when we have proven to be faithful in the little things, but we also gain confidence when we've been successful in them. Remember, young David graduated from the bear, to the lion, to the giant.

*Never be afraid to trust an unknown future to a known God.*

### CORRIE TEN BOOM

*"'Master,' he said, 'you entrusted me with five bags of gold. See, I have gained five more.' His master replied, 'Well done, good and faithful servant! You have been faithful with a few things; I will put you in charge of many things. Come and share your master's happiness!'"*

### MATTHEW 25:20-21 NIV

*Don't dwell on what went wrong. Instead, focus on what to do next. Spend your energies on moving forward toward finding the answer.*

### DENIS WAITLEY

## POWER UP

*What "stage" of your journey are you in?*

_____

_____

_____

_____

_____

# WHAT IS YOUR DREAM?

*Dreams are the touchstones of our character.*

HENRY DAVID THOREAU

All across the country, as I meet leaders, one question I enjoy asking them is: "What is your dream?" You can tell a lot about a man's character by the substance and size of his dreams. They speak volumes about his motives, priorities, values, purposes, and goals.

*If you can imagine it, you can achieve it.*
*If you can dream it, you can become it.*

## WILLIAM ARTHUR WARD

*Praise the Lord, my soul, and forget not all his benefits . .*
*. who satisfies your desires with good things so that your*
*youth is renewed like the eagle's.*

## PSALM 103:2,5 NIV

*When you believe in your dream and your vision, then it*
*begins to attract its own resources. No one was born to be*
*a failure.*

## MYLES MUNROE

## POWER UP

*What is your dream?*

_____

_____

_____

_____

_____

# MAKE A GOAL,
# MAKE A FUTURE

---

*The most important thing about having goals
is to have one.*

GEOFFREY F. ABERT

---

Simply possessing a goal will put you in a higher league than most of your peers. I remember J. C. Penney once said: "Show me a stock clerk with a goal, and I'll show you a man who'll make history. Show me a man without a goal, and I'll show you a stock clerk." Goals make the difference between dreaming and doing.

*Good things happen to those who hustle.*

## CHUCK NOLL

*. . . forgetting what lies behind and reaching forward to what lies ahead, I press on toward the goal for the prize of the upward call of God in Christ Jesus.*

## PHILIPPIANS 3:14 NASB

*Success is the progressive realization of a worthy goal or ideal.*

## EARL NIGHTINGALE

## POWER UP

*What is your latest goal?*

# FROM THE INSIDE OUT

*Some people change jobs, mates, and friends, but never think of changing themselves.*

We live in a generation consumed with changing exteriors. We've bought into the notion that if we just can change the people, circumstances, and environment around us, we can solve our problems. Most of the time, however, the issue lies within us. God doesn't hold us responsible for what happens to us, but for what happens in us.

*When an inner situation is not made conscious,*
*it appears outside as fate.*

**CARL JUNG**

*Examine yourselves, whether ye be in the faith;*
*prove your own selves.*

**2 CORINTHIANS 13:5**

*To improve is to change; to be perfect is to change often.*

**WINSTON CHURCHILL**

## POWER UP

*Who or what acts as your barometer for when*
*inner change is needed?*

_____

_____

_____

_____

_____

# TAKING CARE OF BUSINESS

> *If you see a snake, just kill it. Don't appoint a committee on snakes.*
>
> H. ROSS PEROT

So much needless red tape exists in many organizations. I hate red tape. I agree with Ross Perot when it comes to the "snakes" of life. If we know what the "bottom line" is, then we can clear any obstacle that prevents that goal. Often, we don't need any further research or discussion; we simply hide behind it because it looks like positive action. Look for ways to realistically solve problems. Activity does not always equal accomplishment.

*An ounce of action is worth a ton of theory.*

### RALPH WALDO EMERSON

*". . . be as wary as serpents, and as innocent as doves."*

### MATTHEW 10:16 NASB

*There are risks and costs to action. But they are far less than the long range risks of comfortable inaction.*

### JOHN F. KENNEDY

## POWER UP

*How do you handle obstacles when they come up?*

# THE HUMBLE LEADER

---

*Lord, when I am wrong, make me willing to change; when I am right, make me easy to live with. So strengthen me that the power of my example will far exceed the authority of my rank.*

### PAULINE H. PETERS

W hat a fitting note to conclude with. This disarming petition forces me, as a leader, to adjust my heart as well as my head. When all is said and done, I want the life I model to speak louder than the degrees, ranks, and titles I may have earned. After all, when my journey is over, I want my leadership to be who I am, not merely what my job description says I do.

*There are good leaders who actively guide and bad leaders who actively misguide. Hence, leadership is about persuasion, presentation and people skills.*

## SHIV KHERA

*Create in me a pure heart, O God,*
*and renew a steadfast spirit within me.*

## PSALM 51:10 NIV

*Humility is the gateway into the grace and the favor of God.*

## HAROLD WARNER

## POWER UP

*Reflect on the benefits of humility in leadership.*

# ABOUT THE AUTHOR

J ohn Maxwell is one of the world's most respected authorities on leadership and personal effectiveness. He has written more than a hundred books, including the *New York Times* best seller *The 21 Irrefutable Laws of Leadership*, which has sold more than 4 million copies. In addition to his writing career, he is a popular speaker, inspiring more than 250,000 people annually at appearances nationwide.

Dr. Maxwell's advice is based on his thirty-plus years of experience as a pastoral and organizational leader. He is founder of Maxwell Leadership, an organization that helps people maximize their personal and leadership potential. He has served as a senior pastor for churches in California, Ohio, Indiana, and Florida.

Dr. Maxwell lives in Atlanta, Georgia, with Margaret, his wife of more than fifty years.

Additional copies of this book and other titles
from Honor Books are available online.
Also available from this series:

*The Power of Thinking Big*
*The Power of Leadership*
*The Power of Attitude*
*The Power of Influence*